MY PET

Hamsters & Gerbils

Jane Burton

Belitha Press

First published in the UK in 2000 by
Belitha Press
A member of Chrysalis Books plc
64 Brewery Road, London N7 9NT

Paperback edition first published in 2003.

ISBN 1 84138 082 2 (hardback)
ISBN 1 84138 354 6 (paperback)

British Library Cataloguing in Publication
Data for this book is available from the
British Library.

Editor: Claire Edwards
Designer: Rosamund Saunders
Illustrator: Pauline Bayne
Consultant: Frazer Swift

Printed in Hong Kong

10 9 8 7 6 5 4 3 2 1 (hb)
10 9 8 7 6 5 4 3 2 1 (pb)

PDSA (People's Dispensary for Sick
Animals) is Britain's largest charity which
each year provides free treatment for some
1.4 million sick and injured animals of
disadvantaged owners.

A royalty of 2.5 per cent of the proceeds
from this book will be paid to the PDSA
(People's Dispensary for Sick Animals)
on every copy sold in the UK.

The products featured have been kindly
donated by Pets at Home.

Contents

My hamster

whiskers

ears

front paws

tail

claws

My gerbil

ears

tail

whiskers

claws

It's fun owning your own pet.

Hamsters and gerbils are fun to have as pets, but they are small and easily frightened. You should treat them gently and look after them carefully.

Hamsters and gerbils need feeding every day. You will also have to keep their homes clean and make sure they are happy and healthy.

Young children with pets should always be supervised by an adult. For further notes, please see page 32.

What is a gerbil?

A gerbil is a little animal that looks like a mouse. It has strong back legs, long feet, little front paws and a long tail.

Gerbils are very lively and curious. They like to explore and scrabble around.

Most gerbils are brown, but some are grey, white, gold or black. Some have stripes or patches.

Gerbils like to live in groups. Never keep one gerbil by itself.

What is a hamster?

A hamster is a little bigger than a gerbil. It has a small stumpy tail. Hamsters sleep for most of the day and wake up and play in the evening.

There are lots of different types of hamsters.

In the wild hamsters live in deserts. They sleep in burrows under the ground.

Some hamsters are very small. Some hamsters have stripes or patterns on their fur.

Some hamsters have long hair. They look cuddly but they need to be brushed a lot.

Gerbils and hamsters make nests for their young.

When a gerbil or hamster is pregnant the mother makes a nest out of hay, straw, or special paper bedding from a pet shop.

Gerbils and hamsters are born with no fur and their eyes closed. Young hamsters and gerbils drink their mother's milk. This is called suckling.

When a mother is feeding her babies, she needs lots of water, fresh milk every day and extra food, such as cheese or egg.

Hamsters and gerbils are ready to leave their mother at about six weeks old.

Your pet will need a place to live.

Hamsters and gerbils can live in a cage or a tank. This hamster tank has a nest box on top. The cage below has two nest boxes. It has a clear lid that fits on top to stop the animals escaping.

Put a deep layer of wood shavings in the tank or cage for your pet to chew and dig in.

Your pet will need some
nesting material. Put
in some hay or paper
bedding from
the pet shop.

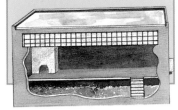

Give your pet some toys to play with.

Hamsters and gerbils will enjoy playing with toys such as this tube. Never give them metal toys or anything painted.

If you let your pet out of its cage, shut all windows and doors. Watch your pet all the time – hamsters and gerbils are very small and very fast.

You can buy toys from a pet shop, or make them. Keep toilet rolls or half a coconut shell for your pet to explore.

Gerbils like to dig underground. Make a hill of wood shavings so that your pet can burrow into it.

Give your hamster an exercise wheel. Make sure there are no gaps in it or the hamster might trap its foot. Gerbils do not need a wheel – they prefer to burrow.

You will need to look after your pet.

Give your pet a piece of hard wood, a special gnawing block, or a brazil nut in its shell to chew on. This will help to keep its teeth sharp and short.

This gerbil is listening out for danger noises. Gerbils and hamsters have very good hearing and do not like loud noises. Do not keep them near a television or a music speaker.

If your hamster is asleep, don't wake it up. It needs to sleep during the day.

Never use cotton wool, knitting wool or bits of clothing for bedding. It may tangle round your pet's legs, or your pet may try to eat it. Never use newspaper as the ink will harm your pet.

Your pet will need fresh food every day.

Give your pet special hamster and gerbil food in the evening. Clean out any old food. Do not give your pet too much food, as it will go mouldy.

Put the food in a heavy dish so that your pet can't knock it over.

Give your pet some fresh fruit or vegetables every morning. It will enjoy carrot, apple, pears, grapes and tomatoes, but not lettuce. Wash all fresh food.

Make sure your pet
has fresh water every
day. Put the water in
a special drip feeder
rather than a bowl.

Hamsters carry food
around in their cheek
pouches. They also
like to store food
in their bedding.

You will need to keep your pet's home clean.

Remove old food from your pet's cage or tank once a day. You will also need to remove droppings from your hamster's cage every day.

Clean your pet's home once a week. Empty out the floor covering and put in a fresh layer.

When you clean your pet's home, wear gloves, or wash your hands with soap and warm water afterwards.

Once a week, put in some new nesting material for your pet, but do not throw out the old nest.

Once a month give your hamster's home a spring clean. Your gerbils will need this only every three months.

Wash the cage or tank with soapy water and special disinfectant. Make sure it is dry before you put in new flooring and nesting material.

Be gentle with your pet.

Your pet will be frightened when you first pick it up. Move slowly, and do not reach down from above. Offer your pet a piece of food and talk to it quietly.

Do not squeeze your pet or hold it by its tail. Stroke it gently from neck to tail.

When you are handling your pet, sit or kneel, or hold it on a table. If your pet does fall and you think it is hurt, take it to a vet straightaway.

Be careful if you hold your finger out to a hamster. It may think it is food – and bite!

When your pet is tame it will enjoy running from one hand to another. It may run on to your shoulder and up and down your arm.

Help your pet stay healthy.

Hamsters and gerbils groom themselves
to keep their fur clean and shiny.
If your pet's fur looks dull, or if your
pet has runny eyes or nose, you may
need to take it to the vet.

If you feed your pet well and keep its home clean, your pet should stay healthy. A healthy animal has bright eyes, a smooth coat, and a clean nose, bottom and ears.

Your pet needs lots of things to gnaw on. If its teeth grow too long, it may not be able to eat properly. If this happens, take it to the vet, who will file your pet's teeth for you.

Your pet may become ill if its cage is in a draught, or if it is kept too near a radiator or in direct sunlight.

Hamsters like to live alone, but gerbils like to live in groups.

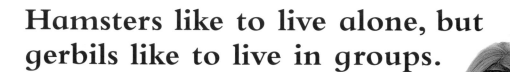

Gerbils and hamsters should not be kept together as they will fight. Hamsters also fight each other, so it is better to keep one hamster by itself.

If a hamster has toys, and you play with it every day, it won't get lonely.

Gerbils live in groups in the wild, so one gerbil on its own will be lonely.

Always keep two
gerbils together.
Make sure they are
females from the
same litter, so that
they are happy
together and do
not have babies.

Gerbils enjoy living in a tank filled with
a mixture of moss, earth and chopped
straw. They can burrow
into the earth.

Your pet may live for several years.

Hamsters and gerbils may live for up to three years. As your pet gets older it might lose its fur and put on weight. Make sure you do not feed it too much.

If your pet escapes from its cage, do not chase it. Close all windows and doors. Put out some food and wait. Your pet will come out to eat and then you can scoop it up gently.

If you look after your pet carefully and treat it gently it will have a happy life. But just like people, one day it will die.

You may feel sad when your pet dies, but you will be able to remember how much fun you had together.

Words to remember

bedding Soft straw, hay or special paper for an animal to sleep in. Also called nesting material.

burrow To dig underground.

desert Land where there is almost no rain.

gnaw To chew something with the front teeth.

groom To brush an animal. Animals groom themselves with their paws.

pouches Spaces in a hamster's cheeks where it can store food.

suckling When a hamster or gerbil drinks its mother's milk it is suckling.

tank A glass or plastic container that can be used to house a gerbil or a hamster. It should have a tight-fitting lid, but allow air in.

vet An animal doctor.

whiskers Long fine hairs that grow on an animal's face.

Hamsters and gerbils grow quickly

A day-old gerbil.

A gerbil at one week old.

Gerbils at five weeks old.

A hamster at three days old, suckling.

Hamsters at 14 days old.

Index

Notes for parents

Hamsters and gerbils will give you and your family a great deal of pleasure, but owning any pet is a responsibility. If you decide to buy a pet for your child, you will need to ensure that the animal is healthy and happy. You will also have to care for it if it is ill, and supervise your child with the animal until he or she is at least seven years old. It will be your responsibility to make sure your child does not harm the gerbils or hamster, and learns to handle them correctly.

Here are some other points to think about before you decide to own a hamster or gerbils.

- Hamsters and gerbils should be six weeks old before leaving their mothers.

- Hamsters sleep during most of the day and should not be disturbed. If this is going to be frustrating for children, gerbils may be a better choice of pet.

- Hamsters and gerbils must not be kept anywhere too hot or too cold. If hamsters become too cold, they may go into hibernation and die.

- You need to have space to keep the gerbils or hamsters indoors. A hamster cage or gerbil tank should measure at least 75 x 40 x 40 centimetres. A gerbil cage should be at least 60 x 25 x 25 centimetres, but varies depending on how many gerbils you keep.

- Do not keep female and male gerbils together. Hamsters should be kept on their own.

- When you go on holiday, you will need to make sure someone can care for your pets while you are away.

- If you have cats or dogs, keep them away from hamsters and gerbils. These little animals are easily upset and can become ill from shock.

This book is intended as an introduction only for young readers. If you have any queries about how to look after your pet, you can contact the PDSA (People's Dispensary for Sick Animals) at Whitechapel Way, Priorslee, Telford, Shropshire TF2 9PQ. Tel: 01952 290999.